EMBARK
PAINTED
ROADS

EMBARK PAINTED ROADS

Adam Conkey

Published in the United States of America.

ISBN 978-0-615-71951-1

Embark painted roads.

Why must it spin away and with such speed?
The faster you go the faster it leaves,
And into horizons the world recedes.

I have come far but I go farther still,
To suns I must see with lungs I must fill,
If even the night I must course I will.

But not all have come with purposes pure,
Some travel idly to only procure,
A likeness for those too timid for tour.

These painters they come with color and crime,
To steal that image I sought all this time,
To crop and corrupt in a frame sublime.

No color can capture that moment shared,
Between the self and the serene unpared -
Only memories of where one has fared.

Travel we thus and embark painted roads,
Not color of art but of paces slowed -
Portraits of places your sojourn is owed.

Introduction

I have not written this book to tell you about anything in particular, or to try to convince you of anything, or to teach you anything. I have instead written it to share something with you. This book is a collection of thoughts that I had recorded in my notebooks somewhat sporadically over the course of four years. I initially had no intention of ever publishing these thoughts, and it was only until very recently that I decided to do so. There was one feature of my notebooks that pushed me to make them publicly available.

When I read a good book, say a novel or a book of poetry, I am constantly anticipating that one passage or poem that knocks me to the ground. I will read the whole book and will be attentive throughout, but the majority of it is read with a sort of passive understanding. What I am really doing is seeking out that stretch of words that will melt me, the passage that I somehow identify with, the block of text that seems as if the author had me in mind when he or she was writing it.

I found that when I read back on my own notebooks, I could not get up off the ground. I was constantly being leveled by what was written there. This is, of course, because the author was me, and I always have myself somewhere in mind when I am writing. I could always identify with my own writing because I knew exactly why each entry was written. Most were written out of necessity, a need to get a pressing concern out of my head and onto a sheet of paper, and therefore reading back on my notebooks was often quite a moving experience.

I was convinced that my notebooks would only have such an effect on me. I assumed that any other reader would find them to be largely incoherent. This is just a feature of how I tend to write. I write for myself, so I rarely accommodate my entries for other eyes. I will often cut straight to the thought or the emotion or the sensation that I feel compelled to write about without introducing it or even indicating what I am writing about. When I later look back on an entry I wrote, I do not need the introduction, for I know precisely what I wrote about, why I wrote it, and often even where I was when I wrote it and the circumstances of my day at the time it was written. Given the lack of context that pervades much of my writing, I did not see the value in exposing it to the public eye.

But I then realized how I read books, as I indicated earlier. I cannot relate to much of what any author has written, but there are portions that I understand fully, and in this way I draw a line connecting the life of the author to my own. It was the realization that my own writing could have this effect, that others might read what I have written and understand fully what I was writing about without me even having to tell them, that made me want to publish this book.

There is a more general feature of our creations to be noted. We do many interesting things to try to express how we are living. We write books, poetry, we sketch, we paint, we take photographs, we sing, we play music, we sculpt, we tell stories, we act, dance, we create films. We do any number of things to provide others with something they can interact with in order to better understand what we are personally experiencing. All of these forms of expression are wonderful, but they are fundamentally deficient, for not one of them can do perfect justice to the first-hand experience each was intended to capture.

Our experiences are hopelessly private. We may sense that another is experiencing at least something similar to what we had once experienced, but we cannot be sure. It is unfortunate that we cannot empathize strongly enough to breach that barrier experience has built up around each of us.

We are not so alone though. We have this arsenal of art forms to wage war on our experiential walls. If you paint me a picture of your loneliest night, it might just bring me back to my own night of perfect isolation, and I might understand what that night was like for you. I will write you a poem as I am basking in a day of sunlight and cheer, and you might read this poem and recall the day you spent free of your own persisting concerns.

You can see that if we have lived similarly in any way, and we try to capture what we have experienced in some form or another, we may develop a line of communication that is beyond the sharing of mere descriptions of our private lives. We will not simply tell one another what has happened, we will enjoy a mutual understanding of the seemingly individual experiences we have.

Of course, in order to avoid merely describing to one another what we have done or merely presenting one another with a beautiful piece of work that displays what we have experienced, we each must live. In order to have a mutual understanding of some occurrence, we each must experience that occurrence for ourselves.

This is not to say that everyone should be doing and thinking the same things; having a perfect understanding of every individual life is not possible and is in fact not even desirable. We are all different people living different lives, and it is that way out of necessity. This world is far too complex and diverse to be enjoyed fully by any one person. This is part of the reason why we require our forms of art and expression: we need to share what it is that we are experiencing because each of us cannot experience it all first-hand. The other part is the part that I have been pointing to throughout this introduction: our art ensures us we are not alone in what we do.

This particular book is perhaps not of the sort that you are accustomed to reading. It consists of an eclectic bunch of entries concerning a range of subject matter. You will notice some conspicuous themes and recurring thoughts, and I think that is good, for then you have some indication as to what I worry about most. If you do not see anything you like in the first few pages, I ask that you press on at least a few more, or even jump around until you find something that interests you. For such a random, seemingly incoherent book, there is a lot that is said, and I hope that you come upon at least one entry that you identify with.

I thank you for picking up my book to begin with, and further for even reading this far. That you were interested enough to do so is a compliment I will accept, and I hope that you read on.

I will send you on your way with one final remark. We should constantly take to each other's lives with fascination. Every one of us is profoundly interesting in our own way, and to learn of what others are doing with their time is itself time well spent. But, do not forget that you have a life of your own to live, and that you must make it extraordinary. We are all obliged to live a great deal, and to speak proudly of it. We only insult one another when we live otherwise.

Adam.

November 2012.

Note to reader:

The traditional book structure with parts, chapters, sections, a table of contents, an index, and coherency ended for this book with the introduction. From here on out you will find only entries, ranging from one line phrases to multi-page essays. This is how I write so it might as well be how you read. There is also no discernible order or organization. Thoughts resonate with us most when we do not see them coming, so wander the woods of my words freely – I have left no paths for you to follow.

I awoke today to discover that things were not as they were when I had left them the night before. I was no longer myself, and my surroundings were no longer my own. I sat on the edge of my bed for minutes? Hours? I will never know. I was trying to make sense of the change, but I was secretly trying to undo it.

I failed. On that bed I was a stranger, one the room had never met and the room one I had never seen before. Some changes cannot be undone. I came to accept this fact, but I was still wanting. I needed a good reason as to why I had been exiled from the familiar. I questioned the walls, the bed, the body I now found myself in.

"What has happened here?" I asked. "What has changed from one waking day to the next? When may I return?" No answer.

I left the room and entered another. This room was identical to the last, yet entirely distinct. It was familiar, but foreign still, and in a different way than the previous room. I sat down on the bed and began my interrogations:

"What is your relation to the last room? Why do I not belong here? Where is my bed from last night?" No answer.

I opened the door to the next room, again identical, again completely unknown to me. I began running through these rooms, each room with a bed and each with a door leading to the next. In each room I asked my questions, and in each room I received no response. Panic entered with me in one of these rooms, and together we ran frantically from room to room searching for the life I had been so abruptly abandoned by.

We came upon one room different from the rest. It was identical to all the others, save one feature: there was a body on the bed. It was me. Panic waited at the door.

Here I was, from the night before. I could not delay: "What has happened? Why am I so different from you?"

Finally something that speaks. "You are worried," he said calmly. "Do not worry, we are not so different. You see," he explained, "each night as you sleep, a new room is built. And each night you are carried into the newly constructed room and placed on the bed. In the morning you wake to a world you have never seen before, and you are left to discover it. You often don't even notice, and we have a good laugh about that."

"Wait," I interrupted his chuckle, "what do you mean 'we'? Who else is here?"

"Oh yes," he said, "I forgot to introduce you to the others."

He walked over to a familiar looking door and opened it. Through it I could see room after room, all identical, all with a door open to the next. And I saw in each of them a familiar face: my own. As the rooms stretched on, each face was just a little bit younger, and a little less aware of what was going on.

"You see," he continued, "every day you wake up a different person in a different place, and each night you join us in preparing the world for the next. Every so often you notice in the morning that something has changed, like you have today. On these occasions we get to meet you sooner than the night, and it is a joyful time."

You might think I would be dumbfounded by all of this. I was not. I was relieved, for here were individuals that had all woken once to a strange place, and they all survived. What is more, their strange places were now perfectly known to them, and they had such great stories. I told my new friends I must be brief, and that I would see them again when night falls – I had a strange place of my own to get to know. I bid farewell and hurried back to my newly built room.

Once there I opened the window, climbed out, and here I am. My world is so vast and unknown, to think I have delayed this long in meeting it. But I had to tell you the truth before I ventured out. Now you need not concern yourself when you wake as a stranger in your own bed. You simply walk out the window, and live abundantly.

■ □ ■ □ ■

What is it that brings you to where you are now? What brings you to where I am now? Our circumstances are unknowing. They bring us to where we are, and we enjoy what we see when we get there.

■ □ ■ □ ■

This world makes its move by being productive, for productivity's sake. But what is a world worth when one cannot sit and look at it, for its own sake?

■ □ ■ □ ■

There is a subtleness to who I am. It is that thing that hides when I come to share it. It is the thing that I cannot say anything of, because it is the very words that I try to say to you. It is the thing that lives so softly inside of me. But it is not lost to you.

You can see it at night when I have only my songs, or when I am in transit, thinking only my thoughts. You can see it on weekends when I have my coffee. It was once visible when I stood in the distance and admired my way home. You can see it when I am running through a day of sunshine, or when I contemplate the rain that strikes my bare skin. I sometimes even leave it out in the open where it is sure to be seen.

But if you were to search for it today, or any other time of your choosing, you would not find it. It is not that I hide it so well, it is just that you have no idea what you are looking for. No idea.

I am precisely the space between my words, the pauses that get mistaken for a lack of conversation. I am the closeness of my reflection when I am eye to eye with myself, looking for something, anything, that I can fully explain. I am the sound of my voice when I talk myself to sleep, perfecting my mistakes. I am the thought I have when I sense that I am alive enough to know I do not want to be anything else.

It is difficult to find, but no worse than your own. Perhaps one day they might meet, and we can sit and watch them holding hands, satisfied by the impossibility of their collision. This is the only way anyone will ever really meet anyone else.

■　□　■　□　■

The silence of the art is what speaks most loudly to me. It is that volume that prevents me from leaving. Those are the waves that grip the innocent traveler in his way, the waves that beckon him to stay as he is. He wishes his world to be enveloped by the chatter of a still image, the tones that are somehow silent to the others. Hang a collection on four walls and try to leave. Try to even hear a voice out the door, or see a speck of light through the window. Four walls of artful creations are enough to close a door on the world, a tomb built for an aesthete, the traveler renounced. This is where beauty comes to die, and therefore where it chooses to live forever.

■　□　■　□　■

Live so that others might look upon your life and
begin to think about their own.

Together, we look.

What is this land
So barren and dry?
On the ends I search,
Each low and each high.

I look for life,
Not people or things.
For they are not rare,
These people and things.

The life I seek,
So densely contained,
Is in a body,
So beautifully named.

She walks this land
So barren and dry,
Keeping it alive,
As well my hopes high.

I look for her,
Not them and not those.
For they are not rare,
These people and those.

The girl I seek,
So perfectly framed,
Is here in this place,
Unknown but named.

She looks for me,
As for her I look,
And so we shall be:
Together, we look.

A thunderstorm was born on this day, and I was the witness. I knew the rain was coming. The sun was dim and clouds were sweeping the skyline. The leaves of the trees donned that shining silhouette appearance against the sky. I could hear the distant rumble of thunder. On any other day I would have observed these things and guided myself indoors before I was caught in a downpour. This day, however, had me awash, wandering with an inexplicable vacancy.

Instead of fleeing, I stood up, gathered my things, and walked to the heart of the open hill I had been observing. Just moments before, that hill was peppered with sunbathers and Frisbee players. Now it was empty. Just me and the closing storm.

The slight breeze turned to wind in an instant, the dim sunlight to a blanket of cloud cover. I looked straight up and saw a swarm of tiny bugs. They knew something eventful was occurring. One by one, raindrops took gravity as their guide and found their way to the grass surrounding me. It was cold, frigid, like that first enveloping step into a chilly pool, the air simply impossible to breathe. I began to shiver. I could no longer look straight up, the raindrops becoming too large to meet face to face.

At any point in this, the logical thing to do was to get up and run for cover. Instead, I stood up once more, gathered my things, and did nothing at all. I just stood there. The rain poured through me, soaking everything displayed and discreet. I was taken by the spotted pattern the rain made against the deep green trees at the end of the hill. At that moment, I could not be moved. My shivering discomfort screamed for me to go inside, go under a tree, dig a hole, do SOMETHING. But I could not. All I could do was smile. With the birth of a thunderstorm came the death of a vacancy, and my day was saved by the exchange.

■　□　■　□　■

If you must question why I do the things that I do, I have already been misunderstood.

■　□　■　□　■

My Dreamer.

Look to me and my printed fortress,
I spare my attention to a gentle lady.
Glide in your steps past my hopeful gaze,
I will avert and direct it all on a cue.

Speak in a tone that I will notice,
Inaudible is the only volume I hear.
Careful in the colors of your dress,
Most lonesome in the beauty you keep to yourself.

Take to your orbit and let me see,
The path you frequent to be lost in the unseen.
Spare me a glance as you pass my seat,
Avert and direct it so as not to be seen.

I will have noticed your shifting stare,
As subtle as it asked it spoke softly to me:
"I am alone and I need you here,
Do not walk away from a powerless dreamer."

Here I will sit, awaiting your pass,
With my pen to my dreams and my powers to you.
I refuse my feet and as I am,
I'll wait for you dreamer as you come back to me.

The strangeness of knowing you are alive. It is the thought with no expression, as there are no words that meet the sensation in effect, and no action that offers the right combination of appeal and calamity. It is on occasion a thrill, and on others the prelude of despair. Tonight it is a frustration.

The capacity to say what I am feeling being so noticeably absent, the lack of confidence I have in you feeling as I do, even if you say to me we are not so different. What am I to do with such incomplete behavior? What bothers these thoughts are.

They are peculiar though. I never taste the bitterness off on its own. There is a hint of sweetness, the caustic aroma they exude laced with the scent of honey. If I try, I see past the terror, and I see what I am designed to see. I see that I am alive, simply, alive. I do not need to explain it, or justify it, as much as I would like to. I need only see it. I will rest to that sight.

■　□　■　□　■

Here I am again, born over and over again. I had once died, and walked away clean. Through my steps I had witnessed what a life can do, and I brought it upon myself. So much so, I fell to the bottom. I died. And ever again I rise to take another step, to breathe another breath. I will pass again, in good time. But I am always back for more. Alas, I aspire.

■　□　■　□　■

Every so often, I smile unconditionally. Without good reason my smile runs free and the people wonder, "What have we to smile about?" My smile queries with equal puzzlement: "What else have you come here to do?" And everyone smiles, free of condition.

■　□　■　□　■

If you think you can do something, try it. If you think you cannot do something, try it. In either case you might be proved right or wrong, but isn't knowing better than speculating?

■　□　■　□　■

The problem that we share, living and dying all at once. We have seen life happen before, and we will see it again, but not out of imminence. To live, you must find your subsistence repulsive and seek to end it, not by death, but through an excess of life.

There are exactly two limitations each of us must confront: what we are capable of doing, and what we are willing to do. The problem is that the latter is often mistaken for the former. Living, in its proper sense, is action tending toward capacity. It is the process of bringing one's will to the known boundary of human feasibility, holding it over the edge, and letting go. Never be satisfied by subsistence.

■   □   ■   □   ■

A good song is one that stops you in your tracks. Whatever you are doing at the first note stops, no matter how important, and you get swept into it. It is one that you feel, when the last note arrives, that life itself was worthwhile if the only meaningful things to ever occur were that song being composed, and you listening to it.

■   □   ■   □   ■

I am awalk.

I walk. And I walk and I walk and I walk. And I stop. I turn the corner. There are signs EVERYWHERE to tell us what we should and should not do. But none for me, the lawless walker. So bound by your behavior, I am a volitive piece of the earth I cover. The lights do not tell me to go, I only go because you don't. These cracks like chasms I cross in a bound. I can be so large from this view. I am a walking poem on these streets, words with every step.

I walk. And I walk and I walk and I walk. And I stop. But only in the light. Great thoughts were never written in darkness.

I walk. And I stop. There is a time on this street, but I know nothing of it. We are all animals out here. Some more than others. The music keeps my step, but they know nothing of it. If I look up enough, I am not even moving. How far you must walk to get to where you are going. I am so easily blinded, I react quicker than I even know how to. I am the abstraction of the night, all because I think, and walk. I don't look at you. You walk as well, but you are not the night, only yourself.

I walk. And I walk and I walk and I walk. You look at me. I look away. You follow your lines. I avoid mine. Take your lights and light your road. Mine are here to stay. Where else can I be? Anywhere I take myself. I sit. I stop. I go. I change songs – this night needs the depth of a chord so gently played.

I walk. And I cross. I look both ways – this life is too important to me.

I walk. And I walk and I walk and I walk. And I stop.

It is hard to believe that anyone could be satisfied by a fixed life. Even if you were to accomplish a great many things in your life and had pushed yourself to a point where you could rest and live a routine, is anyone really fit to be such an idle character?

The human life so limits us, and there is simply not enough time to live sufficiently. There are always things to do, things to see, things to experience. If it could all fit into a handful of decades, then not a single person would fear death, for there would be no point to living any longer.

Fortunately, our world is so interesting it resists exhaustion by any one person. Even collectively, we only touch the surface. So how can we ever find a plateau to rest on? How is your world not canvased with peaks and treacherous valleys to explore? How can you be satisfied with any distance, no matter how small, travelled at a constant speed? I cannot understand.

■　□　■　□　■

It is unfortunate that we have shrouded a life worthwhile in titles and certifications. You are continually measured by what you have accomplished in your life, but only in what you have done, and not in the sort of person you have made yourself to be. This is evident from our priorities in conversation. I will much sooner ask what you do for a living than I will ask you who you are. Perhaps this is because you will not know what to do with such a question, but this is only because my priorities are not the only ones that are skewed.

I will ask you what you do, and I will infer what kind of person you are. How nice it would be to work in reverse. I will ask you what kind of person you are, and will infer what someone pays you to do with it. This would be a more fruitful interaction, for we are not so quick to change who we are, but we can seamlessly change occupations in a matter of weeks.

If you first tell me what you do and I infer what kind of person you are (and tell you to your face), you might be offended by what I say. I might not accurately describe you, and you will not be willing to force yourself into my description, you will just think I am an asshole.

If you instead describe to me who you are and I venture a guess as to how you make a living, you might find that what I offer is a much more fitting occupation than what you are currently doing and discover a more desirable life to live. If you are sufficiently pleased with what you do, you will simply tell me how I am wrong, and I will not be offended. No assholes here.

You can see that if we triage our conversations differently, we not only cut to what is essential to each of us, but we may help one another in finding what we should be doing that we are not. We should thus care less for our more lucrative pursuits, and focus more on that which is not so immediately apprehensible, that which we can actually have a conversation about.

■   □   ■   □   ■

It would seem I encounter you on a daily basis. You always look different. Still, you are beautiful, insular, and you have an inescapable effect on me. And yet, I always let you walk away.

■   □   ■   □   ■

The uneasiness of your light is enough to put me at ease. You are only as chaotic as you wish to be called – I think your dance is charming.

■   □   ■   □   ■

I often worry about the transparency of my life. I worry that I have perhaps leaked too much information, and in so doing have rendered myself obvious. I fear that I have projected myself too plainly on the public canvas, and that I will no longer feel the joy of surprising someone that thought they knew all there was to know about me.

But I then remember I have not been so generous. If you were careful in browsing the life that I call home, you would notice that some of the walls give a hollow thud when you knock, and some of the paintings hanging on the wall have hinges on one edge. I have deceived you, for I have not told you all there is to tell about me.

It is good to have secrets. If there is nothing you keep covered in the corner, you have given too much. When you have a secret, you have something to look at when the concern of transparency settles in, and you may then reassure yourself that you have not yet been made. Keep at least one thing entirely to yourself, and take it with you to your grave. Just think of how many secrets have lived on in this way. Why not allow yourself one mystery, one fact to forever keep that you alone could ever know?

■　□　■　□　■

If only we could combine our skills. Me, the conscious observer; you, the body of flight. What I would give to be able to move as you do and see what you see. Though I am sure if only you knew, you would wish to move as I do and see as I see.

We are not so different you and I, both in envy of what we will never be. The only difference is in my knowledge of it, and your inability to ever have to worry about such things.

■　□　■　□　■

I do not want to forget that I am lonely, I want there to be no loneliness to forget.

■　□　■　□　■

The stars.

Here is the silence you keep,
Out of your window you see,
There are lines in the stars,
And people that walk beneath them.

Out of the silence comes sleep,
Out of your window you see,
There are only the stars,
And the lines that go between them.

Within the silence of sleep,
Out of your window you see,
There are songs in the stars,
And people that sing between them.

Out of the silence of sleep,
Out of your window you see,
There are only the stars,
And the songs that go between them.

Here is the silence you keep,
Out of your window you see,
There are songs in the stars,
And people that sing beneath them.

It is certainly no accident that the majority of influential figures involved in intellectual pursuits have suffered some form of mental illness. I cannot say I am surprised by this fact. Putting all of your intellectual effort into a single task for any extended period of time will necessarily bring you into some state of detriment. Interesting problems require the unrelenting focus and patience of a discerning mind, and if we are ever to achieve anything in our pursuits, we must travel down that road. What I find most remarkable is our willingness to do so.

We could live comfortably and allow those problems to exist free of our attention, but we do not. We are drawn to them, we accept the discomfort and seek resolution, because we find an answer to be a better prize than the satisfaction of our idle tendencies. We have guts, to say the least. We are bold enough to venture into places our minds are not suited to explore, not in a sense of deficiency, but in that one places one's well-being at risk by seeking answers to challenging problems. I can only express my great admiration for inquiring individuals. They are the bravest of us all.

■　　□　　■　　□　　■

If I could put you into words, I would. I could read you anytime I like, and I might even understand you. I might be able to glimpse a thought or two about me, and I could read them over and over again. I would know you as well as you know yourself, perhaps even better, since I would be but gathering your words and not producing them. But, you escape me.

I cannot capture you in my book like all the rest, for you are still too fresh in my mind. You are in there, living the same moments over and over again. I would never tell you to leave; I like you where you are. I only wish you were here as well, either the 'here' in which I reside or the 'here' in which my ink does. For then I could better ask you what you think of me. Your impressions only have so much to say.

■　□　■　□　■

I know that I love you. But, I do not know you, or who you should be. So I love the thought of you, the thought of someone who can love me.

■　□　■　□　■

The Line.

This world includes a line drawn by rooftops,
A demarcation to separate my world from the rest.
Of lines I am expert,
I draw them myself.
I live as a man,
But I dream with the birds.
The rooftops drew me a line, and I provided the
     cut,
With a walk I severed the world of below.

My way will be watched with the edge of one eye,
I proprioceive a path for my thoughts to rise
     above.
I traverse and progress,
Transcend and digress.
I move as I must,
But my ideas are calm.
In fact, I do not notice the level of my creature,
For I have long since been one among the birds.

These roads are cramped enough to be left behind,
And these sidewalks, further, will not hold what I
　　have become.
Surfaces so limit,
The ground inhibits.
I keep my feet here,
But I have gone elsewhere.
I have made walks in the sky where they are not to
　　one side,
But cover the whole of where I must wander.

There will be water that runs the walls. I step along the edges of the floor with my hand raised to graze the coolness as its flow from above commences. My fingers spread evenly so as to cause a new path for the passing liquid. Over my hand and down my arm it courses, pausing at my elbow to contemplate its fall to the floor.

I soon press my face to the façade, the water closing one eye. With the other I see the crystalline streams merge to the shape of my arm, my elbow drawing the trickle back to the source. I bring my stomach to the surface. My shoulders form holds for the diving droplets, tiny bowls to collect them before too many have joined and they must be on their way.

My feet inch closer to the base, a streamline is formed on my spine. I feel a chill on my lower back as a ripple changes course to reach a previously protected dry spot. My hair is slowly matted to my forehead, the streams dividing in the cut of my bangs. My ears fill with water and it is clear that I am no longer in my room with a rampant imagination.

I am inside a waterfall, the water rushing around my body forming a liquid mold of a familiar shape. I hear each breath as my lungs continue to work, my heartbeat filling in the interims. My thoughts are vivid, the roaring hush of the falling waves creating a garden of good ideas. I soon begin to feel an emotion I have not felt before. I see a color I did not know existed. I hear a sound I thought I had once made up myself.

I begin to perceive everything around me simultaneously. The ragged surface I have pressed myself against, the glimmer of sundots on my brow, the crash of a completed dive at my feet, the timely caress of a water drop as it slips beneath my chin. I know precisely where I am, what I am, and why I am who I am where I am. The gift of perfect knowledge, bestowed by a wall of falling water, received by me through the attempt to know something other than myself. And here this waterfall has learned from me, as she might understand for the duration of our fusion what it means to be lost in the thought of someone else.

I step back, two bodies as they were, but now each with a previously unknown experience that the other was desperately hoping to share.

■ □ ■ □ ■

Everyone has been asking for guidance on how to live their lives. They would like to know what should and should not be done, and for what should be done, how to best do it so as to feel no pain. I am concerned by how few of us wish to know more.

Does it not seem reasonable to wish to know what it means to live before one asks how it can be done better? It is this widespread ignorance that worries me (I would call it indifference, but it doesn't capture the failure to notice there is a question worth asking that is not being asked). I want people to wonder what they are, and to not be so convinced by the first answer they were given before they learned how to think for themselves.

I find it hard to believe that, if you continue to question and to reason without a bias by your side, you will not approach something of a similar appearance to what I have come upon. It is not to say that I am right absolutely, it is to say that there seem to me to be natural conclusions to draw when you think your way through to the end.

If this place were better understood, I would not take as much issue with how people are living their lives. The freedom of volition should come at a price. It should be earned by first acquiring the knowledge of what this is all about and what, as a human being, you are. Too many have been helping themselves to a liberty that, as a child grabbing snacks from the kitchen counter, they did not know was something they were not yet supposed to have.

■　□　■　□　■

If I were not alone, if I had you here, I would look to the stars and ask you what you think of them. Would you wonder of what they are? Would you ask me how they got there, how they will leave? Will you wonder instead of what *you* are? Does their appearance make your size seem different to you now? Perhaps you will tell me you once lost your way while walking among the constellations and you had to ask them for directions. Maybe you are a dreamer. Maybe you know too much. Maybe looking is enough, and my questions are out of place here. I wonder what you would say about those stars.

■　□　■　□　■

The melancholic mistress.

Darken the roast.
Darken the sky.
Darken the day.
Open the door for the melancholic mistress.

Welcome the wit.
Welcome the wag.
Welcome the droll.
Open a chair for the melancholic mistress.

Gentle her voice.
Gentle her touch.
Gentle her breast.
Open your arms for the melancholic mistress.

Temper the pang.
Temper the pain.
Temper the ache.
Open your heart for the melancholic mistress.

Listen to woe.
Listen to rue.
Listen to grief.
Open a song for the melancholic mistress.

Adore her charm.
Adore her grace.
Adore her mood.
Open the day for the melancholic mistress.

(...)

Because her heart is dark,
It is beaten not beating,
She deserves no love.

Because she is somber,
She is broken not breaking,
She deserves no love.

Because her gaze is low,
It is sunken not sinking,
She deserves no love.

                    Here she is, lovely, lost,
                    The laconic and listless,
                    She deserves my love.

                    Here she is, beaming, brash,
                    The ballistic and boisterous,
                    She deserves my love

                    Here she is, moving, mild,
                    The melancholic mistress,
                    She deserves my love.

I suffer the disease of indecision on the largest of scales. I do not wake up and wonder which pair of pants suits me best on that particular day, I wake up and wonder which life I should wear until I die. I do feel pressured to make such a decision. I have been coerced into making such decisions my entire life. Every day I am implicitly encouraged to select the project I am to carry out for the rest of my life. The issue is that I cannot make such a choice, not because I am unsure of what I want to do, but because there are simply too many things that I want to do.

This life tears my limbs in all directions. I cannot settle on one project, one career, one path. I want to sample them all! And I am afraid, being only a single man, that I will never experience them all to the extent that I want. This is a fact. Come the end of my life, I will inevitably walk out with a tinge of regret, for there will be some aspect of this life that I was unable to explore properly. This is a more general feature of trying to squeeze an infinite object into a finite space: something ends up spilling to waste on the floor.

That being said, I will still be the over-packed traveler, the guy stomping on his suitcase at the gate trying to fit just one more item into it before he departs.

This world disposes me to indecision, so I may as well embrace that and allow my indecision to guide me through this infinitely interesting world that I find myself in.

■ □ ■ □ ■

I am not one to argue for what I believe to be true. I am not out to convince anyone of anything. The appeal of my words will only strike those who have already snuck a glimpse of the world I have come upon, or those that feel the world they have come to know is the result of profound misunderstanding.

It is misunderstanding that colors the panoply of human endeavor. We are plagued by our fallibility in trying to make sense of what, where, when, how, and why we are. But at some point, you simply grow weary of answers. Answers are cheap. Once you have gone through enough of them, you begin to wonder, of what value are veritable responses to your most pressing questions?

I may, on some days, wish to know precisely what it is that I am, and what is my status in the world. But on the others, on the days when I have the time to send my mind to the places it is restrained from visiting, I no longer wish for truth. On these days I wish for something much more basic: I merely want to feel, what it is that I feel. I do not ask questions on these days, nor do I try to answer others. I just walk. I breathe. I see things, hear things. I am deeply aware that I am a living thing, and an impressive one at that. I sense that regardless of what I am, I am something between everything and nothing, and that is enough for me.

■ □ ■ □ ■

It does not matter how much you learn of your place in the world, or of the complex composition of your existence; you will feel the same weight of it as if you knew nothing of its nature at all.

■ □ ■ □ ■

I am off in the poetry of a task, one so simple, no one of good sense would employ me to do it. Its simplicity is precisely what prevents its exploitation, its uselessness its own protection. Of course, it is of great use to me. I will not live off of it, but I will live because of it, and that seems a sufficient utility to me.

■　□　■　□　■

What is this unbearable desire to live? Why do I sit and ponder the incoming rays of incitement, the common calls to bring myself to the actions of a desperate moment? I am too provoked to simply sit, too restrained to simply act. This gets me nowhere.

I would like each moment to come and go with purpose. I would like to have every conviction restored to the force it was born with. I would like to see where these thoughts would take me if I just let them be.

■　□　■　□　■

Life is distinctly vibrant. Everything is lively.

■　□　■　□　■

Where in your delicate storm you
sheltered the wind

From feeling the pain that you do.

There is an awareness in you I have not seen.

For lack of a better face,

You have come here to see the world.

What will impress you?

Nearly all of the people that I will encounter in the next twenty years are somewhere in the world at this very second, doing something. What fun it is to entertain the thought. Of all those people, one of them, I hope, will be the girl I come to love. This thought is unbearable to me. That she is out there somewhere at this very moment, and that her somewhere does not coincide with my own. What is keeping us apart? What am I to do that could bring you to me sooner? I look forward to making your acquaintance.

I can say, I already love you, and I always have. Let us meet so I can tell you to your face. I may also tell you that I have missed you, even on our first 'hello', for I miss you already, and such a feeling is not known to diminish over time. Do not be alarmed if I stare. Moments from afar are always so carefully drawn, I will not know what to do with the thing when it is placed before me. And if I seem at a loss of words, it is because I am. I spend hours brewing eloquence, but such beautiful language I save for the page I will write you when I think later of how we met.

When that event takes place, I will not be thinking in words, and I will therefore have nothing to say to you – you will see it all on my face. And I am not so unskilled that I am unable to read an expression when I see one I like; I have been waiting for yours for years. Let us live this moment soon. Waiting only makes us suffer together while staying so far apart. If we are to suffer, let us at least do it with your hand in mine and mine in yours. That is a distance I can accept.

■   □   ■   □   ■

The edge is in fact a ledge no wider than the heel of my foot. On this ledge I am alive and well, inching my way with a spectacular view. But if I am not careful, if I gaze too long at the open air or if I allow my confidence to run free, I will see what is below first-hand.

Conscious life brings with it a terrible burden: the knowledge of certain death without a hint as to when it will actually occur. Even if you do not fear it, you still must think about it, and how that thought will not grow into a fear is beyond me.

■   □   ■   □   ■

The way.

I have come to these streets,
Only to lose my way.
Two roads and four turns,
Only one to be made,
And you ask me which is the way.

I can tell you to turn,
But only with ideas.
No signs no landmarks,
Only chance to amuse,
Yet you question which is the way.

I will tell you the way,
I am not such a tease.
You're on it, and I,
Only go as you please –
To there and from here is the way.

Try to live for the briefest of moments without any sense of meaning in your life. You do not have any purpose for being alive, you are not on course to pursue any effort – either self-defined or handed to you – you are not a part of a greater scheme that you fail to fully comprehend. You are, in the greatest sense, alone in the boat, left to your own devices. There is no action that could be of any importance to you. Live with that thought, just for an instant.

This is how people kill themselves. They get too close to that thought, and are not prepared to gaze at it for more than a few seconds. I toyed with the thought once when I was trying to paint my picture of the world. I quickly colored it in disguises and pretended to keep knowledge that I was, in fact, too afraid to witness. But I now look at this thing, this thought that I am in every sense alone, and I can almost stomach it.

Nothing I do, or can do, can ever have any lasting meaning in the sense of having some eternal effect or permanent significance. Any relative meaning I produce – meaningful to me while I live, meaningful to others while they live, meaningful to humanity while it lives – immediately collapses to nothing once I consider the thought of the previous sentence. This is the scary thought that intrepid souls must look upon. I have already peeked and stared for too long. It now grips me.

There are many reactions that I am not going to have to seeing this thought. I will not pretend I have not seen it. To do so would only exacerbate the desperation I feel. I will not insist living is just a futile exercise and end my life today. That would be assuming I know all there is to know. I will not sit in defeat and bide my time by counting the days 'til death do us part. That would just be a more painful version of ending things now. I will do none of these.

What I will do, is invite this hideous thought into my home and welcome it to join me for breakfast. When we are satiated we will walk the streets, spending the late morning and early afternoon in the sunshine exploring the potential reasons for being alive. We will eat lunch by the sea, and ask that body why it churns today as it did the last. We will find bicycles to navigate our way home, and question the wind that is only felt when the wheels are spinning. We will prepare a meal straight from the earth to taste the pleasures a completed life may bear. Sunsets, silhouettes, silent songs and sung ones too – these will make our evening company. In the moonlight we will read the labors of our fellow loners and run with them to the night where we part to rest, only to greet again in the morning.

I will live each day with that thought, allow it to pervade my waking existence until I am indistinguishable from it. I will not live in fear, in regret, in avoidance, or in doubt. Why doubt what you can never be certain of? All I may do is live a life, a human life, and see what it affords. All the worries of what sort of life that may be and whether or not it is the right one must be left at the start. We must come here, take pleasure in this wonderful existence, and let it be on its way. Whatever may fill that time is completely up to each of us, and must be only as significant as it seems to be.

Do not shy from this thought – its harshness is only in appearance. What is wrong is to pretend that you never saw it was there, or worse, to never go looking for it to begin with.

■   □   ■   □   ■

Like chasing daisies in an ice storm. I endure this cold and lonely journey, and there is but one thing that keeps the sound in my steps: that speck of color in the distance. So far away, but in sight none the less, it is that glimmer of difference that makes the struggle at hand a justified course of living. I do not need fields, thriving gardens, I find hope in that lone flower of afar. I long to feel the gentle brush of the petals, to smell its sweet fragrance, and to lie beneath the few rays of sunlight it enjoys.

What of the frigid air I now breathe? What of the sting of slanting rain upon my face? What of the puddles in my shoes and the wind through my clothes? I am one impervious to it all, for I have my daisy in the distance.

■ □ ■ □ ■

Dear, you must look at the view. It is incomplete, but we paint by day and pencil by night. Our colors, they are new, never before seen. And our shapes, they never sit still. Details are but details, it is the view that captivates. Dear, look at our view.

■ □ ■ □ ■

I thought I was distancing myself from these struggles of mine. They were becoming infrequent and lacking in severity, all was well. I see now that they were simply being avoided. I can set myself in the public eye and appear a social dabbler splashing about the puddles of people, but it is only to distract myself from what I naturally must face.

The avoidance only makes the confrontation more explosive. Instead of a daily sorting of issues, I allow them to gather momentum inside of me until there is no containing them, and then the outcome is tragic: self-combustion. Attention to the building burden is key in this life.

■　□　■　□　■

I move forward with a certain expectancy of error, failure, hardship, bottoming out. But when any one of these things actually happens, it is as if I had never seen it coming.

■　□　■　□　■

Body of all troubles kept.

If only a body were all my problems met,
A solid sentience I could meet with my own.
I would face this body and would tell it my name,
And soon then thereafter the first swing would be
      made.

I would thrash at this body of all troubles kept,
Batter it and bruise it into hours unknown.
No weaponry would I draw, no sights would I
      aim,
My rage is enough to need no gun and no blade.

I would torture this body 'til like I it wept,
'Til it begged my forgiveness through cries and a
      moan.
With that one final gasp I would finish the maim,
I would kill all my troubles, to death they'd be
      laid.

If only my problems were in this body yet,
To rest I could lay the distresses that have grown.
But alas I suffer and will do so the same,
No body is my troubles, and none can be made.

It is when I feel out of place in the most familiar of settings, this is when I am concerned. When I sense a lack of understanding in every expression I meet. This is all too improbable though, I know I must not be alone. Where are you?

■　□　■　□　■

Thinking deeply is seen as a deviation from daily activity. You are not to allow your thoughts to venture too far from your surroundings, lest you be taken for one of the depressed, or one of the emotional ones.

Is it a fear? Are you afraid that by walking the darkened roads, you will not return? Do you look timidly at these avenues because the Idles walking about the lighted corridors have told you to avoid that which you cannot see clearly when the night falls?

Night has just fallen. Where do you stand? Are you reading maps beneath a streetlamp, figuring a shorter route home, or do you loiter in the moonlight, no further from home than when you began? What thought can lead you astray when you had nowhere to go from the start?

I walk the roads with no lights. It is lonely out here, but I am not discouraged, for if there is anything that will bring traffic to these streets, it is a testimony that one may travel them and still be able to find one's way back. And I may say, you will not only find your way back, you will return with treasures of the dark, and oh how they astonish with delight.

■　□　■　□　■

I do love a good rainfall. Not always while I am out in it trying to get to a warm place, but when I am fortunate enough to have a patter on a pane of glass. It is cleansing, a washing of the surroundings, as if the earth could not wake without its morning shower and cup of coffee. The rain does not always seem so innocent – it is the adversary of another day. But when you can see it means no harm, that each of those drops is as delicate and fickle as you, you cannot help but appreciate the quiet company.

■　□　■　□　■

You can be so protected when you stand in isolation. You may move to the center of the room and burn from the top down, the inside out, right down to the floor, and you will spare all but yourself. Perhaps you do not want to see anyone but yourself feel pain. In particular, you do not want her to feel even a slight discomfort, whoever she may be.

But when you put two of these burning beings next to each other, it is clear that a tragedy shared is a tragedy enjoyed. Side by side they burn top to bottom, inside out, but here their disappearance is anything but a solemn affair.

They face one another, the flame of one weakening the walls of the other, and vice versa, the contents of each struggle pouring into the other. Soon even they together are not enough to hold what their encounter initiated, and their gentle thoughts flow out into the world.

They burn together so closely, so brightly, they are still distinct but becoming less so as time proceeds. Two lovers losing their lives, but doing so with smiles upon their faces. They need not live forever, they will just as well leave at this very instant. What matters is that they do not burn alone. They will go down together in the magnificence of shared affliction, each one vulnerable to the treachery the other has allowed them to see.

To burn as a pair is the ending of every perfect love story. A story of no regret, no remorse, no lament in seeing what two bodies become when they move to the center of a room and spare all but themselves.

■ □ ■ □ ■

Leave me to my night where the sounds lay down the day, and me a man of despair, chained to my seat with a head full of intentions and weathered thoughts.

■ □ ■ □ ■

Loose thoughts like loose change. They are so small and light, and I find them in the strangest of places. And yet, I find my pocket is just too weak to carry such weight. So I put my thoughts where I am sure to find them once more, if only to create another strange place.

■ □ ■ □ ■

I am nothing stationary. I cannot be sure what it is I am accomplishing, nor can I clearly state what it is I wish to accomplish. But I am doing. I am fighting motionless at all costs, and I will not even slow down to give it a tease.

■　□　■　□　■

Whispers and tip-toes are not welcome here. I want explosions in these skies. Holding yourself together in a neatly bundled package and living your life are notions at war. Do not worry so much about preservation, worry more about running short of time to live profusely.

■　□　■　□　■

Expertise is not my expertise. Not even a desire. I would sooner be rookie at most everything than to excel in just one. Thus, mediocrity in abundance: a soul teeming with ordinary, yet existing as anything but.

■　□　■　□　■

Our footsteps loud and coming.

We haven't the time to play wasteful cards,
Or to have listless talks,
Or to make tasteless jokes,
Or to eat common foods,
Or to have passive fights,
Or to give halfway hugs,
Or to learn routine songs,
Or to take tepid baths.

We have only time to breathe,
Our passions in between us,
Our livelihood for offer,
Our footsteps loud and coming,
Our grievances unrestrained,
Our silences unprovoked,
Our rainfall made for shivers,
Our embraces made for warmth.

What could you ever hope to understand about me when you have not yet felt the softness of the night? What can you say of what I have become when you have not entertained the loneliest hour of the day?

Gentle sounds, gentle lights, gentle songs, gentle sights. You must stop at this instant, and do not think. Do not do. Do not take possession of anything. Do not make a sound. Close your eyes. Listen to the way you breathe.

At the bottom of each breath, there is a pause, a sliver of tender thought that courses the aging night. In that pause, you will find the softness I speak of. As you become familiar with that pause, that softness, you will become familiar with me.

■ □ ■ □ ■

In a world of boundaries, I have been tipping the most salient of the bunch, only to find I was the one who had built them to begin with.

■ □ ■ □ ■

This man is gone, he has left us. In living his course he was taken by an idea. This idea, once conceived, does not let go. It grips the man as he wakes, walks with him through the day, and occupies him as he sleeps. Ideas as such are rare, but they are genuine, and they cannot be controlled. What remains is a sovereign thought, and the man that labors to its desire.

There is a repetition of thought this idea inspires, and it plays for the man when he contemplates what he must do. "Must" is appropriate, for this idea enters as a necessity and never recedes. This man now belongs to this idea, he is entirely lost to it.

Let us not mourn, but rejoice in losing once more a fellow to the discretion of a thought.

■　　□　　■　　□　　■

When I come across people that excel in what they do, to the point that I cannot even fathom how they came to such a level of existence, I naturally question: "Why not me?" Not in a "woe is me" sort of way, but I question what characteristics this person has that I am lacking that allow them to live so proficiently. Certainly some develop their talents more naturally and at a younger age than others, but is there anything preventing me from developing those skills, period? I do not think that is the case.

The only reason I am not able to develop any particular skill is because I have not yet applied myself appropriately to the attempt. We often claim we were not born to do certain things or we lack a certain trait necessary to obtain some skill, but is it genetics that is to blame, or our own lack of focus? Perhaps our fear of what is not already demonstrated to be possible?

We avoid lifestyles that are unfamiliar to us, perhaps never even seen before, because we are afraid of living in error, afraid that it might not be possible to live in this way or that. Extraordinary people exist only because they once made an attempt at something that others were too timid to try for themselves. So, whatever you are conceiving of at this particular juncture in your life, give it a try. It is in this way that we continually keep our definition of possibility in revision.

■　□　■　□　■

You are.

You were my vision.
The sight I had when I once closed my eyes.

You told me to care.
The love I uncovered when I once held the door.

You had me believe.
The trust I enlisted when I once left the ground.

You started the hope.
The bridge I invented when I once took a step.

You made me think.
The tales I dreamt when I once stopped to rest.

You set me to action.
The dares I encouraged when I once made a fist.

You bid me to run.
The fear I unsettled when I once went too far.

You put me away.
The hiding spot I found when I once was alone.

You gave me time.
The ages I collected when I once took a walk.

You tendered me art.
The self I penciled when I once learned to draw.

You taught me romance.
The heartbeat I lost when I once smiled at a girl.

You offered me direction.
The compass I stole when I once turned the
     corner.

You leveled my routine.
The banalities I gave up when I once predicted my
     day.

You insisted I bargain.
The treaty I signed when I once was in error.

You brought me joy.
The head I lifted when I once was carried away.

You are.
The life I lived when I once took the day.

The room is dark, save the sole lit candle sitting on my desk and the ambient street light that spills onto the floor through my open window. My tea steeps, the quiet aroma filling the air just above the rim of the cup. It is damp outside, perhaps even lightly raining. I am sad. Not because it is raining, but because it is such a familiar and frequent state. I hide away in my lofted space and watch the world below; just another night. But I have this candle, and this tea, and that makes life tolerable.

Sitting with this scene now reminds me I have not come so far. But who is to say progress must come only with a change of habits? I like to be alone, and I like simple things. It would seem then that my scene is not so blameworthy. These greater or lesser moments are all that I have, and even the most deplorable of the lot deserve a pause for reflection, reminiscence even. I will grow to new days and spend them in different places, but there are some spaces I will never leave, and these are the ones that most aptly reveal who I am.

■　□　■　□　■

I am the poet, and I know where I belong. We have built rooms to protect us from what we are unable to predict, as well as the unpleasantries that we foresee. A roof will keep us dry, a wall will stand to the bluster of a wind, a floor will keep the calluses from our feet and the insects on their side. Rooms were built to keep us safe.

I, the poet of dark, will have nothing of it. I will prefer to sit on a stone at the water's edge and admire the ceiling that never starts. I will surround myself with the creaks of a dock, the echoes of unknown companions, and the shadows of bodiless shapes. I will make friends with the elements and stare down a rain cloud with a smile upon my face. The only cover that suits me is the cover of the night.

You may build your rooms as high as you like with comforts I cannot even fathom – I will only walk out of them. The poet belongs to the street: the only home anyone ever left when they walked into their house.

■　□　■　□　■

Yes, even we cannot escape our gravitation. Our orbits are near, they in fact cannot be another way. But it is not gravity that is at issue, it is the repulsion embodied in our inabilities. We are hunters, but hiders as well. Unashamed, yet modest. Amorous, but respectful. We are in trouble, because the force of gravity is so weak here, and we have been counting on it exclusively.

What has strength is volition, courage, a disregard of expected behavior. With these we may be of use to gravity and not, as we do, work against it.

Attraction to us has been more of a fate than a flaw; we cannot ignore what we are drawn to. We can, however, work in opposition to what we feel we *should* be doing, and therein lies our fault. Of course, we are not the only two to blame. We are plagued by living at the whim of probabilities, of chance, of good fortune. Who we are nearly seems to be inevitable, but our encounter is on the opposite end of that spectrum: it seems nearly impossible.

That, is a fault we do not have to claim as our own. We do not own up to a mass improbability, we simply accept it as a course of living. All we can say is that we do things, and that we do not do others. That combination works for or against us, and we can never really be sure which side we are playing to.

What we must see though is that we do not behave by the numbers. We are not captives of chance, the numbers work for us. They at least must listen to what we say, for our actions determine how the probabilities will end up. If we must then pick a side, I have made up my mind: I choose gravity. I work so that we might one day end up in the same room, at the same time, and with the same idea. Do you, similarly, labor with a force of nature? Have you also chosen to favor the draw, and not the repulsion?

■   □   ■   □   ■

Despair does not show itself because I have thought of death, or of my futility, but rather from noticing the world in which these realizations must be made. It is not what I am in itself that troubles me, only being what I am in the world that I was born into.

■   □   ■   □   ■

There is a particular peace on this earth to be felt by each and every individual. It will not be found in the company of any other, nor in any of the comforts that civilized living has come to offer. It is found only in the landscape. In the silence of the breeze on a hill in the cloudless sky there is a thought that everyone should come to know sooner in life than later.

You must think you are as much of this earth as anything else. The man with the massive brain – the brain that barrages him with a sense of grandeur and entitlement, that creates infinite beings for him to answer to – that man is the same man that sits on a tuft of grass and gazes out on a scene in which he is just an extra. This world was not created for man, and once here we do not govern it. We are only playing our part in an otherwise indifferent character. If you sit on your tuft long enough, you can see this clearly.

The landscape may be riddled with the signatures of those coming and going, but there is always one inhabitant that never moves an inch. And so, neither do we. Paint yourself into your picture of nature and try to see things any differently.

■　□　■　□　■

Turbulence. Agitation. Disturbance. Frenzy.
Instability. Unrest. Tumult. Tempestuousness.
Turmoil. Commotion.

The state of my incorrigible mind.

■   □   ■   □   ■

Whatever your pain, know that you are not
alone. Also know that it will pass. We get caught
in our troubles, so much so that we see no hope of
coming back. But it will pass, I swear. Head up,
open eyes, you are bound to see something that
you like.

■   □   ■   □   ■

I am putting sticks to spokes. I am doing
something that I have no desire to do, simply
because I can. Let the wheels seize.

■   □   ■   □   ■

Your mind can be anywhere you want it. Your
body can only go where you put it.

■   □   ■   □   ■

The swaying of a train.

There is a reality to the swaying of a train,
A nonsense it will not tolerate.
A person will get on, another will leave,
The train will just move to the exchange.
It of course needs the coming and going,
But it pays it no attention.
It is here, and so are the people,
And we each do what we must.
Necessity has an unspoken language,
One we all understand without having to learn,
We know every dialect.
We will each sway with our traffic,
But we know at the end what we have come here
    to do.
You have been beckoned,
As the train has been asked of its purpose,
And you must answer as you have decided.
Tell me where your swaying has taken you.
Tell me what you have come here to do.

I know there is a girl out there that is much like me. There is nothing in itself that precludes her from meeting the right people. She is kind, funny, caring, beautiful, but she likes to be alone. She is lost in her passions, and does not know how to leave, or even if she would want to. It troubles me that she is real.

I am angry that I am unable to locate her, saddened to know she is alone. She does not want to be alone, she only cannot help but to live in such a way. This is what makes my present time and place such an infuriating coordinate to occupy.

I want to be with her and she wants to be with me. We are in the end left to wander, searching aimlessly, and with little confidence. But, I suppose as long as we hold true to our ideals, we will one day each swerve in the right direction. Do not forget I am here.

■   □   ■   □   ■

I am wrong to be here in this state. I only know no other way to live.

■   □   ■   □   ■

I caught you in the act. A small note so carefully placed upon the glass. And yet, it happened as if you yourself did not even notice it. You did not even care to look around to see who might be watching. I was watching. By chance, really. I glanced in that direction just at the right moment. Now I sit at a distance. You have long since gone, but your note remains, and so do I, just the two of us. I am staring right at it. And the mystery is killing me! What the fuck does that thing say?! It could be anything at all. An advertisement, a poem, a phone number, a blank piece of paper. ANYTHING! I must know what it says. I am at least too careful, I have been looking in all directions for several minutes, just to see if you will appear again. Perhaps you want someone to find it. Perhaps you want to see who the lucky finder is. Of course, as careful as I am, I am also an impatient detective. I am getting that note.

you are most
BEAUTIFUL
when you are
fully YOU.

A curious fact of the introverted, no one can ever know who we are. You will never really know who I am, you will only be able to relate to me.

I will never be able to fully express my thoughts and desires to anyone, but certainly one can sympathize with my character and sense what it is I cope with. I know what physical and mental isolation feels like, and I can sense when others embrace such retreat in their own lives.

It is this very manner of living, this withdrawal into ourselves, that prevents us from ever becoming acquainted with one another. It is a choice to live this way. We could live otherwise and do our best to disguise the recluse that inhabits each of us, but who can you be honest with if you cannot first be honest with yourself?

Isolation is, however, no more than a pretense. Anyone who chooses to be alone is understood fully by those who live similarly. You will therefore never find yourself completely alone. There will always be others just like you that keep you in sight with an eye of understanding.

■　□　■　□　■

There is a tendency to think of salient figures in our human history as people above and beyond anything that any one of us could ever be. Revolutionary ideas are often portrayed as flashes of brilliance from superhuman minds, but I gather that this is rarely, if ever, the case. Pick up a biography of any prominent intellectual and you will find that they struggled greatly with whatever problem (or problems) they were trying to resolve. Certainly in some cases there may have been a single burst of inspiration that gave rise to the final solution, but there is a long and arduous prelude to such a moment that rarely receives proper recognition.

What distinguishes great intellectual figures (and all other types of outstanding individuals for that matter) is that they were first taken by an idea that they could not ignore. Many people have made very successful careers for themselves by actively searching for the big idea that would make them a star, but the greats were sufficiently captured by their problem that they had no choice in the matter. This is the first step to revolutionizing some feature of your world: find something that captivates you beyond explanation, and succumb to it.

Our revolutionaries were also impressively industrious people when it came to addressing the ideas that consumed them. They could not be bothered by anything else when they were bothered by their idea, and this undoubtedly led to many sleepless nights and days built from exhaustion. Much must be sacrificed in order to pursue anything with the effort you are capable of, but when the pull is strong enough, there is little to convince you that you are doing anything wrong. You must thus convince yourself at times that work is better than play, and try to conflate the two when you can.

Above anything it is important to recognize that every great idea came from a *human being*. Those that shocked the world with their ingenuity were fundamentally no different than you and I. They once lived a life just as we do now, and many of the activities they took part in were no different from the ones that we currently do. They ate meals, they talked casually with friends, they went shopping, they had awkward moments with strangers, they had to pay bills, they went to the bathroom, they laughed, they had all of the seeming trivialities of an ordinary life. All that set them apart was what they placed on top of all that:

their great idea, and the struggle that went along with it.

When viewed in this way, it seems that any one of us might change the world if we simply follow our passions where they take us. I believe this is how it works, so let us get to it.

■   □   ■   □   ■

Be mindful of the picture that passes before you.

■   □   ■   □   ■

Even a day doubled over in dreary thoughts will be sunny out my window. Here the lights rush to the entrance and pile through into my room as if the fire were outside, and the alarm is sounding. I can watch them fighting their way to me, jostling their neighbors, leaving them in the lurch. They do not care to notice how the world burns out my window, they only want to escape it. I let them in, but their entry prevents my exit. Save yourselves from the fire outside, I will just sit and watch the world burn.

■   □   ■   □   ■

The vessel undoing.

Alone with the ominous looming,
Awalk in the deep city brewing.
Tether these clouds to a sky full of light,
And I will here keep on moving.

Amiss with the natural fuming,
Adept in the dark city doing.
Temper these winds with the tune of the night,
And I will here keep improving.

Abreast with the deferent booming,
Aboard in the vessel undoing.
Tell her these storms are the end of a plight,
And the waves will soon be soothing.

I find the most modern of comforts to be the most stifling to my existence. Put me on the bus, in the car, the luxury of a plush seat on my bottom and the buzz of my fellow riders, and I cannot gain a breath on the receding oxygen I struggle to inhale. Place me on the streets with an open breeze, the passing rain, even the numbing cold of an unfair autumn day. Ah! That is my home, that is where I am the lively one. I may inconvenience myself, I may sit with discomfort more than most, but I am oddly all too comfortable with that. I will, without hesitation, take my comfort over yours.

■　□　■　□　■

Apathy is cancer of the soul. Learn to confront a single facet of your life with force, challenge its inhibitions and limitations until you no longer notice the tears it has animated. Seek to conquer a single task and the rest will follow, for resolution spreads, not as a cancer, but as a contagion of impulsion that brings to surface the will to actively affect every detail of your life.

■　□　■　□　■

Paint me in regret. Wild colors, streams of lighting orange – I can only breathe. In. Out. In. Out. I wish it were different. I wish I were different, only exactly what you need me to be. But I cannot pretend to be any other man. You will let me stand here beneath your window while I whisper the things I should be breaking my voice over. I will sit with my eyes enclosed and just breathe. In. Out. In. Out. Pencil me the lines I want to hear, whisper those things you should be keeping to yourself. Shatter my ideals! Break me wide open and see what you see. That is me in there, and it is not all bad. But you are gentle, those hands too delicate to go so far. I wish we were different, but we just never were.

■　□　■　□　■

Love manifests itself as the underlying motivation in all endeavors. Something so simple as buying a cup of coffee. There is an ever-present hope that perhaps today is that day. Today I might look up and see her looking back at me with an expression that sighs with relief: "finally."

■　□　■　□　■

Nature has pressed, and so have I, and the blooms have come out for us both. There are bubbles beneath the surface, trapped and hopeful. One by one they burst without ever seeing the open air above.

But they do not think of it like that. They endure the space and think of that moment when they will slip past the filter and rise to the plane of the fortunate. There they will carry on as they did in the depths, but they will not think of where they will be, they will think of where they have been, and of where they are.

■   □   ■   □   ■

I am nostalgic for a time and place that I do not remember, and in fact can only imagine, for I was not there. Nobody was. I miss the world before the mortar, the motors, the mortals. This world was not wrought with mankind's contraptions and misguided thoughts. It was simply a place in which things happened, free from observation, much like most of the universe carries on today.

What I would give to be the lone witness to this world. I might walk with the sound of my footsteps, uninterrupted by the distant rumble of automobiles and airplanes. I might sit in the dirt and not feel that I am deviating from some standard of living. I might see the landscape in full flourish and not the calibrated scenery left for me in outlooks and overpasses. I might stand in the center of a storm and not fear the destruction it is capable of, for there would be nothing to destroy.

I do cherish the joys of humanity; we have a truly splendid inhabitance here. I nevertheless covet this place of my imagination. It will forever be the place that never was, as far as we are concerned. But it was once real, and that thought alone fills me with joy.

■　□　■　□　■

Indeed, there is peace out here. I have not found it in my thoughts, but I have in silence, knowing that I have thought.

■　□　■　□　■

The sun hides its face, and with it all the people.

■　□　■　□　■

From the trees it rained.

It rains on occasion only under trees,
When they have since lost their leaves,
And the sky has since eased.

The cover I would seek normally from these,
Drips and drops and so deceives,
And so I go uneased.

This world has grown weary of staying the same –
Of coming from where it came,
And doing so unblamed.

And so today the world brought with it a game:
The sky dry did it remain,
And from the trees it rained.

These are the relationships I keep. Quiet, timeless, painful, guarded, exhausting. I never let them see the light of day. I just let them grow in the dark until one day they outgrow that weathered cage I placed them in and the door bursts wide open. But still, I just buy a better cage.

It is no inability of mine to love; it is all I know how to do. And yet it goes to waste. It remains an inaudible sentence that repeats in my thoughts, a silent reminder that I am alone. How can I be so selfish, and yet so selfless? I keep my emotion, my loving attention, my compliments, my care, my affection, my love, all to myself. I keep them here to spare her, because I know they will only hurt her.

It is hard to say if you have ever really been in love. At any given moment you might think you are, any given relationship, only to later find that you were just a portrait of youth, and full of words. Even in a single day, you might convince yourself that she is not for you, and you feel foolish for ever thinking she could have been.

But then you see her, you hear her speak, you enjoy a moment of laughter with her, you hug her, you act a fool just to delay leaving her sight a fraction of a second longer, and you have never been so sure of anything in your life. It is hard to say you are in love, but it is even more difficult to say that you are not.

■　□　■　□　■

I am ashamed of the wisps in my head. Loneliness, attraction, exhaustion, frustration, fear, sincerity, hope, desire, they all just mingle in a whirling cloud that fills the space between the few pieces of clarity I keep. The disorder, the chaos, it disgusts me.

I long for order in my head, a distinct partition of thoughts and emotions. It is all just a mess. It is like trying to grab a fistful of water, and when you pull out your hand to see what you gained, you watch as your prize seeps through the cracks in your fingers. Give me something tangible already! Let me see SOMETHING that ensures me I will not just exist as an abstraction of a human being. Replace my bucket of water with a bucket of snow. Just let me have something to hold on to.

■　□　■　□　■

There should exist chairs in public places that are reserved for interruption. When you sit somewhere, that becomes your personal space. It is implied that you wish to keep to your own business and everyone must think twice before so much as asking if they can borrow a vacant chair.

But if I am sitting alone, might it be that I simply have no one to sit with? Might I wish you would take that vacant seat by sitting in it instead of taking it away?

Solitude is the respite, but at times a sense of hopelessness invades that hangs overhead like a ceiling too sunken to stand under. This state is adjacent to desperation, and on occasion they even collaborate. It is enough to collapse an individual.

One rarely makes it to the ground though. One will instead find oneself fallen into a seat at a coffee shop, surrounded by faces, hoping that just one of them recognizes the sort of day it is. And if this coffee shop had tables reserved for interruption, two kindred loners might meet and make amends with the threats of the day. They could allow their hardships to breathe over a cup of coffee and see the anxiety and anticipation they conceal placed in front of them for once.

It is good to be alone, but not to be lonely. We may cure this fatal illness by eliminating it entirely. Tables for interruption – such a logical solution, I wonder why I am not already seated at one.

■　□　■　□　■

I am sometimes faced with the unbearable desire to do something, but I know not what it is. I am rushed from all sides by pure incentive, a racing provocation with no action to apply it to. This is perhaps preferable to having the need to do something and not possessing the will to carry it out, but it is still an entirely conflicting state of affairs. I can only handle it by squirming in my seat, desperately searching for the action my body has already decided upon. The process is not all that different from electroshock therapy; I imagine I would look the same in either scenario. The only remedy is perhaps to do everything that I have the slightest inclination of doing, until I find that one thing that had covertly approached me with necessity at its back.

■　□　■　□　■

Our Burden.

There was always a worry that I would not make it. It is not that I believed my death to be imminent, it was failing in some other sense that I cannot fully explain. I worried that I was doing something wrong. Perhaps I walked too rigidly, or I could not make proper eye contact. Perhaps I was saying stupid things, just words to form a seam in my unending struggle to find the right ones to say. When they looked at me, I could not stand to watch. I had to look away. I always knew how to act when their backs were turned, but as soon as I could see I was not alone, my walls would collapse. I would sit there in my debris while everyone watched.

It was not always this bad. There were times when I could breathe. I was a builder of sorts. I could make towers, skyscrapers, cars, roller coasters, houses, you name it. They were not toys, they were real, more real to me than anything I could find elsewhere in my world. I was on occasion accompanied by a friend, and that would ease my Burden. It would at least spare me the thought of it, and I could live for some stretch of time without having to worry.

But do not let me mislead you, my concerns were unbearable. A certain anxiety that I took to be my own, I feared that it would one day get the better of me. But look at me. I made it, and I am here with you now. I do, however, come to you filled to the brim with remorse. I am sorry, for I have passed the Burden unto you.

I know what it is that you endure. Your concerns are beyond mine, but I understand them all the same. You are not sure what you are, and this troubles you deeply. You are certain it must be something of a spectacle, but its description eludes you. Your loneliness astonishes you. You just cannot understand how you have made it so far without another to pick up the other side of your Burden, and you worry everyone walks past because they do not care for you. You are not always sure what you should be doing. You worry that you have perhaps gone too far, or that I have guided you wrongly.

I assure you, I have not. You must pick up where I left off. And through it all, do not forget to breathe when you can. You are more of a creator than a builder. You have your words, your songs, your art. You are a walker through the greatest scheme one might conceive of, and this calms you.

If I may guide you any further, it will be by encouraging you. Do not let the Burden take you. Your moments will be wrought with a certain suffering that you will not be able to fully explain, but they will be there, and that is something to be grateful for. You will find many of them awkward, uncomfortable, painful, and even entirely implausible. But, they are moments to have.

I need you to make it so that you can join me in guiding the next. He is waiting up ahead, and he is even more terrified than you. You need to be there to help him along and guide him just as I am going to guide. Listen to what I say, listen to what you want to say, and live in abundance. This is the life we are creating, and we have only just begun.

■   □   ■   □   ■

I will never miss a winter day in my life, for in fact they never leave me.

■   □   ■   □   ■

Seated in a plane high above the earth, you cannot begin to fathom the complexity that you would see walking about its surface. The world as a populated object makes good sense. We may say "this is our place and this is what it looks like", and from our seat such a description does not surprise us. The world as a bustling system of humanity, resonating with distant thought, poetry, emotion, science, families, death, hobbies, art, passion – this we cannot comprehend from the seat up above it all.

And so it may be with our brains. When we are outside considering the brain from a high-level perspective, we say "this is the brain and this is what it does", but we cannot even begin to fathom the complexity that occurs on the level of neurons. We cannot even imagine the incredible discoveries we might make walking about the streets, so to speak.

The earth is our home, but we cannot properly entertain its intricacies when we remove ourselves from its surface. And when we are standing firmly on the ground, we forget the immensity of the system we are a part of. The brain is the engine governing our every thought and movement, but we cannot begin to understand what is occurring inside that gives rise to such pleasures. And when we are situated in a network of neurons, we lose sight of the activities that make us who we are.

It seems we are either in the air, unable to cover the distance from our seat to the floor, or we are stuck to the streets, able to only gaze up at the sky and think it beautiful.

■　□　■　□　■

The observer brings to life everything that is worth living. She sits and records the magic of a moment, seals it in some memory, whether within her or without her, and there the grandeur of life remains.

The world cannot be discovered solely by moving through it, it must also be noted where one is going, where one has been, and what happens to be unfolding in the moment that lies in between these two extremes. Act in your world as it directs you to your place, but also be fond of your seat saved to the side, awaiting a watchful gaze to occupy it.

■　□　■　□　■

I am more or less a ruined individual. Tortured by my inability to form a complete image of what I desire. I cannot settle the temptations, the doubts, the lack of inhibition.

I run with the sorrows of my heart and pierce the strength of my defenses too willingly. My eyes are shut, so I do not see where I am running to, and I am too stubborn to peek. I catch my toes, I lose my weight into some obstacle, I knock things down. I am everywhere in this path.

It is the proper semblance I seek. I want to stand composed and speak a sentence of gold. I want a shining string of syllables to slip from my mouth that says perfectly what it is that I desire. I want to know what it is that troubles me by its lack of focus.

■   □   ■   □   ■

I prefer everything that does not avoid what this is, everything that tolerates only honest confrontation. All else is mockery. All else is a painful realization to me, a devastation.

■   □   ■   □   ■

The heights.

Where this bustling takes us,
To city heights and streetlong walks,
We drive or drive too slow.

The global view from the tallest sight,
It deceives as it makes obvious,
A perspective only fit for the birds.

But even they are not so dumb,
They come from the heights to sit on a stone,
And stammer the infinity of a texture.

When I ask what you have learned, I do not care to know of the books you have read or the facts you have stowed away. No, my question is, what do you think? What does this world answer when you ask it how it became? All of your favorite books were written to respond to just such a question. So, what will others find in your book to stow away for themselves? What presents itself so clearly to you that to think in any other way is to think in fictions? What do you think?

■　□　■　□　■

Content me with a coffee, a candle, with a gentle rain and nocturnes. I will compose you a man who is too far gone to care for you displeasures in life. I read your world with contempt, for I am making melodies that you seem to ignore.

The music has been playing all the while, and I am just now learning to dance. When will the world join me in my unforgettable waltz?

■　□　■　□　■

There is a right answer when I am asked if I have any regrets in my life, if I regret something I have done or a choice that I have made. I say there is a right answer because I am expected to answer negatively to such a question. The right answer is that I have no regrets, that every choice I have made has led me to where I am, and I would not have it any other way.

What bullshit. Of course I have regrets. Do you really think there was not a single juncture in your life that you chose one way when another choice would have left you better off? Can you really believe you are the optimal decision maker?

If you believe in fate, or whatever you wish to call a cleanly drawn plan that you are following, you are wrong. I am not afraid to tell people they are wrong when they are. You are continually tasked to choose and are, in fact, incapable of escaping such freedom. When you reflect on the real game changers, the moments when you felt a fork was paved in the road and you walked one way and left the other to reverie, can you really tell me that you think you made the best choice in every case?

It is true you will never know which was the better choice. You may have been better off if you chose differently, but you may also have been worse off. That uncertainty is precisely what should prevent you from saying you have no regrets whatsoever. There is a great deal of possibility in uncertainty, and to think that you are living the best life of all possible lives seems to me absurd.

I regret because I have made choices, choices that necessarily had alternatives. In hindsight I may look at those alternatives and find them more desirable. It is our curiosity of what could have been that beckons us to regret. I will not be one to avoid that sensation. I will not try to convince myself that this is where I am meant to be. This is where I have chosen to be, and though it is wonderful, I cannot deny that I could have been elsewhere, and that things could have been better.

■　□　■　□　■

And so the winter comes upon me when I enter a decision I must make. What darkness have you for me today?

■　□　■　□　■

I feel a profound emptiness. I glance covertly at you, afraid that you might sense a lonely heart. I wish to speak my loneliness, but I have no words to spare. I can only bring my bones to sit and admire the distance that separates us. All of my energy is consumed trying to close that distance, but I am not as strong as I look. I wonder if you struggle with an equal force. Perhaps we are both facing the current. Or perhaps we are both with the current, just facing the wrong direction. If we just stop trying, let the water course as it wishes and us with it, maybe then we would have but inches to contend with.

■　□　■　□　■

I am helpless to you. Utterly helpless.

■　□　■　□　■

I am embarrassed by my thoughts, but I say them to you anyways, because they were friendly enough to greet me, and I think you might like to meet them as well.

■　□　■　□　■

You know you have come a long way your problems when, one day, after you have struggled greatly and have tried to cope with the frustration, the anger, the sheer disbelief that you could ever get yourself into such a situation, you look at it all and laugh. The scenario you have painted yourself into becomes downright comical, and all you can do, is laugh. Therein lies the secret to growing old: you think as a child and find humor in things that you know you should not.

■   □   ■   □   ■

I am not so graceful coming down from these highs. You build up to your moment from such a distance away, and it comes, it passes, and it is over. The transience kills me. And this will begin again, I will always have something in the making. But I must always return to the largest transient moment I can know of. That moment is long, arduous, and lacking the clear focus of my more modest ones. Such as I go, always in some moment, and never sure how I feel about it until I am in the next.

■   □   ■   □   ■

I have been in touch with the intensity of my existence as of late. The life I bear has been with me in such nearness, I can hardly distinguish my skin from my nebulous involvement.

It is natural for me to worry, to foster anxiety, and fear that I am quickly demolishing the sensible boundaries of my hopeful circumstance. But instead of trying to look away from the building disaster, I stared right at it.

I have not been avoiding the coming and going moments of desperate living, I have been allowing them to pass right through me. And as they do, I listen to what they came to say. I am attentive in the act, I try not to miss a word. It doesn't make the experience any more pleasant, but if something is going to happen to me whether I want it to or not, should I not at least try to get from it what I can?

I do not like to be a mess of emotions and concerns, but I often am, so it seems foolish to avoid or otherwise neglect the predominant character of my being.

■　□　■　□　■

Rubble I must.

Bare to essentials,
Among the things I keep,
I sit in that silence
And think of it all,
All the things it seems I must keep.

I keep them inside,
Where I'm sure not to see,
But feel them I do
And oh how they weigh,
They are much too heavy for me.

So rubble I must,
It's the waste I can't leave,
I stand on that heap
And live with it all,
The things I cannot seem to leave.

There it is, my old familiar foe. Confusion, despair, sorrow, fear. Call it all of the above, I am rarely ever able to define it. I only know it when I feel it. It almost amuses me to think that I play the part so well; nobody knows what goes through my head. And that very fact is often the hardest part to accept. I never speak of it, for I never feel I will be properly understood. Of course, it is all too possible that they play the part just as well.

Perhaps I will just print it on a T-shirt. Most will laugh and ask where they can find such an amusing shirt, but at least one will read it and know exactly what to say, for they have the same one in a different size.

■　□　■　□　■

That of which we are uncertain is what keeps our pace. We press on because there is hope that life will one day be perfect. We blunder all we wish today and reminisce with our naïve selves of the past, but we never come to rest, for there are days we have yet to touch.

■　□　■　□　■

How we shift when we cannot make up our minds. You could say this is beyond me, or perhaps just too far within me, but I have not come so far only to see the point at which I began.

It is that one thought, always that one thought. For as long as she has been there though, she remains nameless. Her face is often new, but never unfamiliar. I have always thought I should be patient with her, for she is being patient with me, but patience to both leaves you both without a name. Someone must give, someone must be impatient.

And that is me, the impatient one. When you live in these thoughts for so long, you nearly forget how to act. You become so fascinated by the speed of the pitches, you forget to swing once in a while. So your steps must be small. Today, it is breakfast sandwiches. Tomorrow, maybe a name. Until one day, that one thought makes for a good story, and she has a name.

You do not always need to have your mind made up, you just need to act as if you do.

■   □   ■   □   ■

Dark when always day.

I stand deep in that unrest,
Sending pebbles to puddles,
But the ripples never reach me.
I could swim all day,
And soon I will;
Only my waves will ever take me.

Now in the swell I am dazed,
Reading old ways on new days,
But the words they never leave me.
I could dream all day,
And soon I will;
Only my eyes will ever stop me.

Is it day when always dark?
Dark when always day?
In this life I know but one.

I will once die,
Once stop moving,
For my days converge to one.

But when I die,
I will die doing,
For in lives I have but one.

Endurance running has, in many interesting ways, trained me for life. I can easily recall the feeling of being in the midst of a race and coming to the realization that there is A LOT left to go before I cross that line. It cripples you. Your motion becomes slow motion, and you want to vomit more than anything. But you deal with it, for you know what is waiting for you ahead: something better, something you are looking for.

And so it goes with my life. I think of all the things I need to do, all the things that lie in my future, and I feel helpless, in slow motion, and I want to vomit just a little. But this effort is worth it, this I am certain of. There are things in my future that are better, things I am looking for. All that is left to do is to get there.

■　□　■　□　■

Having a human body with a human mind, yet never pushing past where you think you must stop. It is like owning a rocket car, yet always going the speed limit.

■　□　■　□　■

You cover my ears and tell me not to listen to them. I listen to you. You take me to places I could not have visited otherwise, places I have been but could not return to, places I did not know were real. So gently you welcome me to join you in your adventure, and I walk willingly in your direction. Take me to those places we do not speak of. I have never smiled so widely.

■   □   ■   □   ■

Eyes. Frightening little things. Furtive glances are all I can muster. It is as if they see something I cannot, like my most personal thought is written on my face and they read with a smirk, a laugh only a breath away.

But *your* eyes. They do not burn like the rest. They are gentle, clear, calming. I look at them and only wish the pixels would give. That maybe, one by one, they would disappear in exchange for a piece of what is real. That maybe I could feel the peace of that gaze as it occurs, and not as a single frozen moment. For me, not the lens.

■   □   ■   □   ■

Strip me bare and there I will be, naked and confused. Let me see your life. I do not want the noise, I do not want the others, I do not want to know of anything else. I just want to know what that life is about. I want to see nothing but the song you sing when you are certain there is only one that will listen. Feel that pain. Suffer. Scream and cry all you want. Only take note, because you are very alive.

■　□　■　□　■

There is this unforgiving compromise between experiencing all of the many ways of life available and experiencing fully any one of them. You can either do a great many things in a cursory and incomplete way, or you can bound yourself to a number any child can count and find what a few activities have to offer when experienced to their full extent.

The decision does not come at me lightly, and I am afraid I have already spent so much time pondering it that I have committed myself to the latter: I have become an expert in indecision.

■　□　■　□　■

This is where I admire the walls for what they are. They are not exceptional in what they do, nor are they even exemplary of what they should be, but they keep the rest at a distance, and there are nights when I prefer the external world to be placed miles away.

These walls enclose a space, and it is here that I leave myself with the questions I can only answer when no one else is watching. The room is cluttered in this way, questions piled in the center, me pacing about the perimeter. If I am feeling particularly bold, I will dive face first to the center of the pile and lie in its core. In the nucleus I suffer.

The walls hide this spectacle from the rest of the world. They secure the perimeter and ensure I embrace the misery of the process. There are, of course, doors and windows in these walls that lead to places, emergency exits for when I am too concealed to carry on in this way. These luxuries are rarely utilized though. I do not wish to avoid troubling things.

Why has the world come to look on trying times with disdain? Have you not noticed that there are unpleasant things, and that many of them reward you greatly when they leave? If you avoid them, they will never offer you anything.

Discomfort in itself is a guest no one wants to entertain, but it is exceptionally rare that this thing comes alone. We find ourselves in grievous states because they are inextricably paired with experiences that require and make the most of us. If each of us passed through this life unscathed, this world would be alarmingly uninteresting, hardly worth looking at. It is the treachery of the uncomfortable that amplifies the sense of living we enjoy, and it is what makes the contrast of contentment agreeable to begin with.

Build your walls when you need them, and leave yourself to distress. There are always doors through which you can walk when it becomes a real nuisance and, if you are a twisted architect, there is always a sledgehammer sitting in the corner, just in case. Allow yourself to sit uneasy from time to time, you will only gain from it.

■   □   ■   □   ■

Overwhelm me by ideas. I have but a lifetime to make sense of you.

■   □   ■   □   ■

The sun does speak.

There is my sunshine
So colorfully made.
In you I seek
A moment of day,
Where I need not speak,
Nor think what to say.

I rest and refine
The habits that grayed.
I have been weak
But not on this day,
For the sun does speak,
It bid me to play.

Regardless of what you are doing right now, where your life has brought you, what you feel it affords you, there is something in this space that you wish to accomplish, something you wish to understand. It is always right there for you, ready to be approached. Do not think that because you have so far only come so far that you are not ready for a proper explanation. This thing is here, and it calls for your attention.

Take to those things that worry you most, and see what you are left with when you have gone any distance in that direction. Your time is too limited to think of any limitation beyond this one.

■   □   ■   □   ■

Taking genuine risks is not in my nature. But I have looked at them from a distance for so long that I have become intimately acquainted with them without even noticing. Perhaps my nature is only what I expect it to be, only what I say it is.

■   □   ■   □   ■

One should find beauty at any speed.

■   □   ■   □   ■

There are thoughts that you are incapable of returning from. Once the thought is conceived, you are forever an exile in your old familiar world, and are similarly excluded from the worlds of others. You do not hope to come upon such thoughts, but intrepid thinkers run the greater risk, and some among us cannot help but to take steps in their direction.

When we stumble, we stumble hard, and become discouraged by our path. We question every motivation we ever followed, every inquiry we ever embarked on. We doubt, because we now face a thought on fire, burning white hot, and we are prone to stare. It is a flame with no extinguisher, and so bright it cannot be ignored. The only course of action is to feed it in hopes that it will burn with such strength, a hole will be seared in the fabric of the world that you know, and you may escape.

■ □ ■ □ ■

I will save you with perfect anonymity. I do not need the credit, I just need you to be okay.

■ □ ■ □ ■

If we are ever to do anything extraordinary, we must not accept our given limitations. We must not compare ourselves to those before us and say "They could not do this, I am no more fit". We must not rely so heavily on inferences.

Failure and success know no faces, and have no conception of time or place. They know not of your experience, your past or present state. All they know is the effort put forth when the attempt is made. All we may do is try things for ourselves and talk of capabilities only after we have seen what we personally can and cannot do.

■　□　■　□　■

There is so much to life that we simply fail to notice. There is power, exuberance, sheer wonder in the world of experience. For too many, it is lost.

This is the state of ignorance, which is nothing more than the act of ignoring all things beautiful. Ignorance should be defined as such – ignoring that which is worth paying attention to, that which is most essential to human involvement.

■　□　■　□　■

Maybe if I sit perfectly still, you will know where to find me. If I look about with my feelings on my face, you will see this is me. Maybe if I were not so diligent, you would be easier to spot. I am always here, always waiting, for you.

■   □   ■   □   ■

I sit in a field of death and decay. Leafless, dry, crackled, and worn. There are no flowers, no streams, no sights, no amusement. The structures are abandoned, and with them the place.

And yet, the sun still shines as it does in the most wondrous of locations. The birds still show up to sing a beautiful song. And the people, they still visit. The sky still opens, and the breeze still wisps. And when that sun should finally venture to rest, those clouds will still ignite into colors I can only recall when I am sitting right in front of them.

The world must change and it will do so with little regard to what is already here, but it will never be anything short of magnificent.

■   □   ■   □   ■

I look at the stained glass, Class of 1941, and I cannot help but wonder about them. Their lives have either reached their end or are quickly approaching it. When they were done, how did they feel about it all? Did they feel they were capable of more, or did they really live to their full capacity? Were they more concerned about themselves, or what they were taking part in?

Their lives are in the books, but mine is very much in the making. And so I may ask, and answer, how do I want to feel about it all? I would like to say I was not a waste. I did not simply observe, I acted as well. I did not idle in the comfort of subsistence, I pushed myself and gave this world something it could use. I endeavored with the best, for they knew as well as I that this is something worth our effort.

There are many things outside of my control, but there is one that has always been in my hand: my desire to live; my will to give a shit. And I do, give a shit.

■　□　■　□　■

She is always with you.

Live for it.
But it's nothing you can have.
Think for it.
But it's nothing you can have.
Long for it.
But it's nothing you can have.

> She is always in the process.
> She is always in the way.
> She is always with you.

Wish for it.
But it's nothing you can have.
Listen for it.
But it's nothing you can have.
Look for it.
But it's nothing you can have.

> She is always where you are.
> She is always where you lie.
> She is always with you.

Scream for it.
But it's nothing you can have.
Lose for it.
But it's nothing you can have.
Love for it.
It's all that you can have.

> She is always on your mind.
> She is always on your side.
> She is always with you.

Should I be so unfortunate as to be inexplicable? Can you tell me in good conscience that I, of all things, am the ineffable one? I am to be explained away with all the rest. I set myself the observer of it all, when I know in my restless evenings that I am as much the object of my observation as anything else. To think that I am somehow different from it all, something above, beyond, below even – absurdities.

Everything that I hold as my own, right down to the 'I' that carries it all, is to be explained in such a way that we need no special universe to let these things be, only our own. Will 'I' be any less real in this universe – in our universe? I will not. For understanding the causes of my self will not serve to diminish it, or delete it altogether from this world. I am quite real, as real as they come. A proper explanation will only reinforce that.

■ □ ■ □ ■

The only absolute truth is our inability to know anything of it.

■ □ ■ □ ■

We sacrifice a little here and a little there to get to where we set out to get to. These sacrifices, though small, add up, and they sink in when you are not prepared to notice how they have piled high. But in time you stop viewing the pile as a burden and begin to see it as a means to climb. When your goals are good ones, you will find the value of that which you give up to be just that of what you wish to find.

■   □   ■   □   ■

Your love does not hear what you say, it will act as it pleases. If you say "go", it will be patient. If you say "stop", it will be swift in motion. Faith is trust in that which you cannot control. Human emotion – therein lies my faith.

■   □   ■   □   ■

In my mental collapse, I saw only you, standing there in the rubble wondering what all the noise was about.

■   □   ■   □   ■

Have you asked or have you been asked lately how you would like to die? Did you answer faithfully? Perhaps you would like to die doing something you love. Are you then willing to die prematurely to die at the hands of a passion? Perhaps you would like to see this thing to the end and die of old age. But do you want this in itself? Do you wish to simply deteriorate naturally and see how this process can be prolonged?

It seems to me unnatural to want to die so passively, as if you had no say in the matter. I am certainly not proposing any form of suicide – this is not even a genuine possibility as far as I am concerned. I am encouraging each of us to challenge the aging process in its way. Do not take your death as it is handed to you. Test it, taunt it, mock it by living excessively. You should not want to simply wither away, you should want to live until there is just nothing left.

You will have travelled so many miles, your legs will no longer fire. You will have climbed so many barriers, your arms will no longer lift. You will have read so many books and listened to so many stories, your eyes cannot help but shut. You will have thought so deeply that your words will drift into nonsense. Emotionally, there will be nothing left to give. You will have loved all that you can love, and laughed at all that was funny. Tears will no longer be produced. All of the energy keeping your life in place will simply run out.

This is the ending of a life lived vigorously. It is the death of choice. Seek it with all you have.

■   □   ■   □   ■

It is a disheartening moment when you discover your life and the course it maneuvers is entirely predictable. I came upon this fact when lifting my head to see where I was heading, and in a moment's turn I had a wrench in the gears. I derailed the train.

I could not bear the thought of a life so easily apprehended, and what is more, it was directed straight towards a configuration I would not have been pleased by. So, I currently stand in the wreckage, admiring the mess I have made. It is beautiful, a ragged pile of chaos freshly stirred. Wonder at the new life I have created.

■   □   ■   □   ■

Wisdom is certainly no fiction, no happy delusion of older men and women that exploit their impressive tenure of existence by simply telling younger minds that they will understand when they are older. Wisdom is real. I know this because I already have it, albeit a small amount, and only in a limited number of areas. But I do have it. And I know this because I encounter people, some younger and some older than myself, that are in a state of mind that I was once in and that I now recognize as seriously flawed.

Infant musings on life, religion, the human mind, relationships, accidents, meaning, purpose, education, success, existence, obligation – I have thought about all of these things, and I have moved past my initial intuitions. Some of these intellectual paths I have travelled a great distance on, and there is really no other way to get to where I am but by travelling the distance it takes to get here. So, when I see someone distanced on one of these roads by miles in my rearview mirror, I can see that they have a ways to go. In this way I am wise, because I see there are others where I once was.

Of course, I cannot say I am leading the way on any one of these paths. I am certainly miles behind in someone else's rearview mirror. It is even possible that the road loops, and those innocent travelers in my rearview mirror have in fact already been where I am now and are now lapping me. Who really knows? This is perhaps the point to be made: you may be certain of any number of things, but you must admit the possibility that you are wrong, that you have not reached the end of the road.

It is likely that each one of these roads is in fact infinite, and we are simply placing ourselves somewhere along them. That seems to me like a good reason to keep moving forward on any one of them. How much of infinity can one person see? That is the challenge, that is what we are up to.

■　□　■　□　■

There you were, crossing my path. Notebook in hand, a yellow purse, a casual gait. And you were alone. I know the type, I only wish I knew you.

■　□　■　□　■

Poor weather inspires in me a will to be productive. When the sun is shining, I lose all focus. I want to be in motion! It is my childlike instinct to enjoy my time in the sun, and I cannot avoid indulging myself when the outdoors welcomes me so. But when there is a steady rain upon the window, I am inclined to cozy up to my studies and gaze out upon the dreary conditions, my mind encouraged to focus on more intellectual matters.

It would seem I should move to a bleaker state if I wish to get anything done. However, too little sunshine, and too much work for that matter, will be the death of the human soul. We not only need the sun for the warmth and energy that sustains us physically, we further require its cheer to sustain ourselves in spirit.

To anyone who thinks they are capable of abandoning all human comfort and reprieve for the sake of maximal productivity, I recommend a gentle stroll on a sunny day, or a bicycle ride along the riverside in the company of a temperate breeze. If, after, you feel you are still fit for the disconnected pursuit of your passions, carry on my friend.

We are simply not built for pure productivity. We need to complement our efforts with the respite offered by nature and the pursuit of foolish games. How you feel, your condition, determines almost entirely the quality of your work.

■　□　■　□　■

There is a difference between an observer and an onlooker. The onlooker merely sees whatever it is they look upon, whereas the observer enlivens it. The observer defies the boundary of liver and looker and opens the cage door.

There are scenes that are in need of exaggeration, of understanding, of a visit from a lovely language. Some actions are not to be left alone, they are to be understood. If preservation were perfected, all actions would be of this sort. As of now, a choice must be made. Still, a choice is of little consequence when the selection provides the same outcome. All observations are to be of interest, which is to say all actions are of interest when properly observed.

■　□　■　□　■

How do you play so beautifully? A wondrous display of human affliction that sings with the strings, I am powerless to such vibrations. One more note and I will confer myself to your purpose with devotion.

You have me now, a life renounced for any duration you ask. You may be finished in a matter of minutes, but I will lie down in the echo for hours and wonder where I would be if I had not initiated our encounter. When the waves dissipate, I am forced to rejoin the more tangible composition from which I departed. It is there that I recognize the vacuum you have left me with, which is really no more or less occupied than before we began. You are thus not to blame for the emptiness. I am. You were gracious enough to pardon me.

I welcome you back any time, but for now I must return to the void. I am at present all that makes it a space to begin with.

■　□　■　□　■

That time of death.

I died in that moment,
What is left hurts to mend.
But I do not give up,
I do not give in.

I live in this moment,
I cherish the remains.
For in that time of death,
It left me none the same.

Is my torment enough to please me? That I might capture the words strong enough to express the crushing winter of my thoughts, will this be enough? Or am I better suited to speak the mundane and live like a solemn thought never crossed my mind?

Treacherous days are of no waste to me, for even though they are far from desirable, I hold them dearly all the same. When I am further removed from them and am here and there reminded that I once saw the storms one's own mind can bring about, I am ensured that I have lived, and have lived well enough to see them through.

And there the clouds rush away,

   for they know they cannot stay with me.

I am bulletproof, no doubt, but what keeps me from bullets also keeps me within myself. I have been trapped here for hours, chipping aimlessly at my armor, hoping for a ray of light to grace my hand. As I fail, my impatience grows in proportion.

A fury is born inside of me, a raging wind that knows no bounds. It begins to sweep the corners of my dusted chamber. Faster it spins, unpredictable it becomes, the wind is taking control of this situation. Round and round the interior goes, and I am huddled within, submitting to its presence. Soon the walls shake, the bolts loosen, slits of light breach the surface and strike my trembling hands. The armor is coming down. In the spirit of catastrophe, the walls concede to the tornado I have become. Jagged fragments explode in all directions, the bolts liquefy, and the wind escapes.

I must stand alone in the aftermath, obliged to feel shame for acting so impetuously. I should have been patient. I should have thought this through. What have I done? I have left myself entirely exposed.

Yes, I have left myself exposed. Bare-skinned I stand and listen to the whistle of bullets surrounding me, but the sound does not frighten me. It is beautiful. Streaming beams of color warping the air, jet streams of determination, collisions of chance. What I have been missing, what our armor keeps us from.

I may not be here for long – not all of those whistles will make it past me. I will at least meet my adversary before it takes me. I no longer have to fear the slow suffocation of my own defenses. I will fall tragically, spectacularly, a brilliantly played drama that leaves the onlookers convulsively searching for a proper breath. I am going down, and I am taking this whole scene with me. Drop the curtain when I am through.

■ □ ■ □ ■

Afterword

I hope that what you have read here was not entirely foreign to you. If you made it this far without finding even a single stretch of words that you understand fully, then you and I are living two very different lives. I prefer to think, however, that I am not so disconnected from anyone. My experiences, my thoughts, my struggles, my pleasures, these are all unique to me and perfectly private, but I link them to your own with the words that I once wrote, and that you read just now. I know that our words are not simply relayed between us, for we are each human, and as such have much to talk about.

We each endure our sentience and know what it means to be alone, to be afraid, to be overwhelmed, to be in pain, to miss an opportunity, to regret, to make a mistake, to be selfish, to be helpless.

We also share many pleasures. We bask in our sensations and are happy, hopeful, in love, liberated, excitable, playful, honest. We smile, we sing, we play games, we laugh, we kiss, we take risks, we do the stupidest things, because we can.

We each must also live with the knowledge that it will all one day end. I do what I can to think (and therefore write) about death often. This is not because I do not fear it – I trembled just now at the very mention of it. Death scares me senseless because I find life to be exceedingly wonderful, and I never once wished for a wonderful thing to end.

I think openly about death because each time the contemplation confirms anew that I live now. When you recognize that what you are doing will one day end, you begin to question why you are not constantly flirting with the extraordinary, and you inevitably start doing interesting things.

I cannot help but feel that that is what this is all about: we are here to do interesting things. I no longer ask what my purpose is in life, what I came here to do. I only ask what will I do next, and how interesting will it be? And I think everyone can benefit from such questions. What will you do next? How interesting will it be?

In the end I hope that this book found you in the middle of something, and at the end of something else, and at the beginning of a third thing. I hope that you have been seeing all that this life offers to you, and that you are not avoiding any of it. Take pleasure in it all and remember it perfectly. Write it all down if you have to, or paint it, or compose it into a song, or a poem, or photograph it, or tell it as a story – do what you must to keep it from being forgotten. I want to know about it when you are done.

About the Author

See the last hundred or so pages.

www.ingramcontent.com/pod-product-compliance
Lightning Source LLC
Chambersburg PA
CBHW050131280326
41933CB00010B/1336